About the Authors

Hi there! We're Margarida and David, the duo behind this book. We're a couple who work from home, juggling two very different jobs, but sharing one big passion, technology and keeping up with the latest trends.

Our journey into Artificial Intelligence (AI) didn't start in an office or through our careers. It began in a completely unexpected place, Marrakech, 2022. While exploring the vibrant streets, we connected with a friendly couple who introduced us to DALL·E. That was our "aha" moment. We were blown away by what AI could create. From that point on, we started noticing how AI was quietly embedded in our lives, whether it was our smart household gadgets or the tools we used at work.

We got so excited about the possibilities of AI, but the people around us didn't always share our enthusiasm. Some of our friends were skeptical, thinking AI was just another passing trend, while others were completely unaware, still clueless about tools like ChatGPT. Fast forward to now, and many of them have jumped on board, seeing what we saw back then: AI is here to stay, and it's already reshaping the way we live, work, and connect.

So, why did we write this book? For me (Margarida), this book comes at a turning point. I'm currently unemployed and finally pursuing my lifelong dream of becoming a writer. In my last job, AI became my secret weapon, I used it to manage meetings, summarize interviews, create impactful presentations, facilitate workshops, do research, and tailor messages for different audiences. I saw firsthand how much time AI could save and how it could make tasks easier and more effective.

And then there's David—with his deeper knowledge of Artificial Intelligence, he brought the technical insights and helped me bring this idea to life. Together, we realized we wanted more people, especially busy families and full-time workers like us, to see the practical benefits of AI. It's not about replacing humans; it's about gaining more time, better organization, and smarter ways to manage your day, finances, and life overall.

This book is our way of sharing what we've learned and how we're using AI to improve our lives. Whether you're completely new to AI or just looking for ways to integrate it more meaningfully into your routine, we hope this guide helps you get on board and make the most of what AI has to offer.

Thanks for joining us on this journey, we hope you enjoy it as much as we enjoyed writing it!

Margarida & David

Table of Contents

Table of Contents — 3

Introduction — 5
   How This Book Will Help You — 13

What is AI? — 14
   Types of AI — 14
      Narrow AI (Weak AI) — 14
      General AI (AGI or Strong AI) — 16
      Super AI — 17
      Generative AI — 19
      Evolutionary AI (Emerging Concept) — 21
      Functional Categories of AI — 21

   A Historical Overview — 23

   AI's Aha Moments — 29

Practical AI in Daily Life — 33
   Managing Daily Tasks — 35
      Virtual Assistants — 36
      Grocery Shopping and Lists — 37
      — 37
      Smart Home Automation — 37

   Finance and Budgeting — 38
      Budgeting Tools — 39
      Automated Investments — 40

   Health and Fitness — 40
      Fitness Trackers — 43
      Workout Recommendations — 43

   Pet Care — 44
      Automated Feeding Systems — 47
      Pet Cameras and Monitors — 47
      Health Monitoring Devices — 48

Travelling	*48*
Automated Travel Planning	50
Navigation and Language Translation	51
Smart Transportation	51
Immersive Travel with AI	52
Jobs & Workplace	*53*
Job Search	55
Meeting Management	56
Workflow Automation	56
Creative Productivity	57
Recruitment	58
Professional Development	58
Making Smart Choices	*59*
Data Privacy Concerns	*64*
What Data Is Being Collected?	64
Steps to Protect Your Privacy	65
The Risks of Over-Reliance on AI	*66*
The Balance Between Automation and Human Skills	69
Addressing AI Dependency	69
Cross-Checking AI Information	69
Ethical Considerations	*70*
Algorithmic Bias	71
Job Displacement	72
Privacy and Data Security: Who Owns Your Information?	73
Autonomy and Accountability: Who's Responsible?	73
The Path Forward: Ethical AI for the Future	74
Algorithmic Bias and Fairness	75
Job Automation and Displacement	75
Future	**78**
Conclusion	**83**
Final toughts	**85**
References	*88*

Introduction

Imagine waking up in a home where your virtual assistant has already set the perfect temperature, your fridge suggests breakfast based on ingredients nearing their expiration, and your calendar reminds you of the day's appointments before you even think to check. This isn't a vision of the future, it's the present, powered by artificial intelligence (AI). Once confined to science fiction and tech labs, AI is now seamlessly integrated into the fabric of our daily lives.

From asking Alexa to set your morning alarm to receiving a perfectly tailored playlist on Spotify, AI is transforming how we live, work, and interact with the world. What was once a complex tool reserved for computer scientists and tech enthusiasts is now accessible to everyone, regardless of age, profession, or technical expertise. Whether you're a busy professional managing a packed schedule or a fitness enthusiast monitoring your health, AI has something to offer.

This book serves as your guide to understanding and embracing AI in practical, meaningful ways. It aims to demystify the technology, showcase its potential, and empower you to harness it effectively. While AI is not here to replace us, it amplifies what we can achieve, boosting productivity, saving time, and enhancing decision-making. Across industries like healthcare, finance, retail, and entertainment, AI is already proving to be a transformative force.

AI Growth and Adoption

The rapid growth of AI has made it a cornerstone of modern innovation. In 2022, the global AI market was valued at $136.55 billion, and it's projected to grow to nearly $1.8 trillion by 2030. This extraordinary expansion demonstrates how AI has evolved from a specialized tool to a ubiquitous part of everyday life.

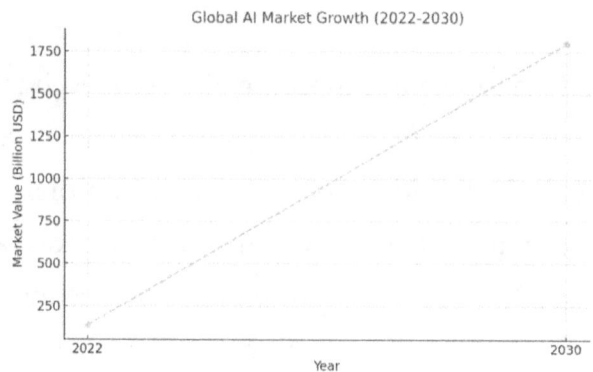

Consider how millions of people interact with AI daily through virtual assistants like Siri, Google Assistant, and Amazon Alexa. These tools manage schedules, set reminders, control smart home devices, and more. AI-powered smart speakers are now in over 120 million households worldwide, and their adoption continues to rise. AI algorithms also fuel many of the online services we rely on. Platforms like Netflix and YouTube recommend content tailored to our tastes, while Spotify creates playlists that feel handpicked for us. Social media platforms such as Instagram and Facebook use AI to prioritize content based on our interests, making our digital experiences more engaging and relevant.

> **AI algorithms** are like step-by-step instructions that teach a computer how to solve problems or make decisions. Just like a recipe tells you how to bake a cake, an AI algorithm tells a computer how to process information, recognize patterns, and complete a specific task.
>
> - If you watch videos on YouTube, the algorithm learns what you like and suggests similar videos.
> - When you search on Google, the algorithm finds the most relevant answers for your question.
>
> AI algorithms learn by looking at large amounts of data, improving over time to make more accurate predictions, recommendations, or decisions.

These tools don't just make life easier, they provide highly personalized experiences, turning everyday interactions into moments of efficiency and enjoyment. Tasks that seemed futuristic just a decade ago are now an integral part of our routines.

AI in Various Industries

Beyond personal convenience, AI is driving innovation across industries, reshaping how we approach complex challenges and revolutionizing traditional processes. Its influence extends far beyond virtual assistants or smart devices.

In **healthcare**, AI has emerged as a game-changer. Imagine a tool that can analyze thousands of medical images in mere seconds, identifying subtle signs of diseases like skin cancer or retinal conditions—sometimes with greater accuracy than seasoned specialists. Doctors are now leveraging these AI-powered systems not only to assist with diagnoses but also to recommend highly personalized treatment plans for patients. Beyond diagnostics, AI chatbots provide round-the-clock support by answering queries and managing appointment schedules, helping healthcare systems provide better care with fewer resources.

The **financial industry** has also embraced AI to simplify complex processes. Personal finance apps like Mint now track spending patterns and help users manage their budgets effortlessly. For those looking to grow their savings, AI-driven robo-advisors like Betterment or Wealthfront analyze market trends and adjust investment portfolios automatically, giving individuals access to wealth-building tools that once required professional advisors. On a broader scale, banks and payment platforms rely on AI to detect fraudulent activity, analyzing transactions in real-time and preventing losses before they occur.

In **retail**, AI is at the heart of the shopping experience. Ever wondered how Amazon always knows what you might need next? Its recommendation algorithms sift through vast amounts of data, analyzing past purchases and browsing behavior to predict your preferences. Meanwhile, big retailers like Walmart are using AI to optimize their supply chains, ensuring shelves stay stocked while keeping costs low. Even customer service has been transformed, with AI chatbots offering instant, tailored support for online shoppers, enhancing convenience at every click.

The **automotive industry** is perhaps one of the most exciting spaces where AI is driving literal change. Companies like Tesla and Waymo are leading the charge with self-driving cars that use AI to navigate roads, recognize obstacles, and adapt to real-time traffic conditions. Features like advanced driver-assistance systems (ADAS), including lane-keeping assistance and adaptive cruise control, are already making driving safer. Beyond the roads, AI is helping manufacturers like BMW implement predictive maintenance, analyzing vehicle data to flag potential problems before they lead to breakdowns, saving time and costly repairs.

In **manufacturing**, AI is revolutionizing the factory floor. Robots powered by AI now handle repetitive tasks like assembly, welding, and packaging with unmatched precision and speed. Quality control has also reached new heights, computer vision systems scan products for even the smallest defects, ensuring only top-quality goods make it to customers. Factories are also becoming smarter, as AI monitors equipment performance and predicts maintenance needs to prevent costly downtime.

Even **agriculture**, a field traditionally reliant on manual labor, is being transformed by AI-driven precision farming. Drones equipped with AI fly over fields, analyzing soil health, monitoring crop growth, and detecting pest infestations. Farmers now have access to actionable insights that allow them to optimize irrigation, fertilization, and harvest schedules. Meanwhile, smart tractors from companies like John Deere automate plowing, planting, and harvesting, increasing yields while reducing labor and resource use.

In **transportation and logistics**, AI ensures efficiency at every stage of the journey. Delivery giants like UPS and FedEx rely on AI to analyze real-time data and optimize delivery routes, saving time and fuel. Cities are integrating AI into traffic management systems, which analyze road conditions and adjust signals to ease congestion. These innovations not only improve commutes but also contribute to reducing carbon emissions.

Education, too, is seeing a quiet revolution. AI-powered platforms like Khan Academy and Coursera are tailoring learning experiences to individual needs. Students now benefit from personalized course recommendations, interactive feedback, and AI-driven tutors that break down complex concepts in ways that suit their pace. Teachers, meanwhile, use AI tools to automate grading and track progress, freeing up time for meaningful interactions with students.

Finally, in the **energy sector**, AI is helping optimize power grids and renewable energy systems. It predicts demand and manages supply more efficiently, ensuring that energy consumption remains sustainable. In wind and solar farms, AI systems analyze weather patterns and energy output, allowing operators to adjust systems for maximum efficiency and performance.

Across healthcare, finance, automotive, and beyond, AI is not just improving processes, it's redefining them. It reduces inefficiencies, saves time, and delivers results with a level of precision that was once unthinkable. While each industry has its unique challenges, AI's ability to adapt and optimize ensures it will remain at the forefront of innovation. Whether it's saving lives, improving commutes, or increasing crop yields, AI is proving to be an indispensable tool for building smarter, more sustainable industries that meet the needs of tomorrow.

A Shift to Personalized Technology
One of AI's most transformative qualities is its ability to deliver personalized experiences. By analyzing preferences, behaviors, and

habits, AI tailors solutions for individual users, turning one-size-fits-all systems into customized tools.

For example:
- **Shopping platforms** like Amazon suggest products based on past purchases and browsing history.
- **Fitness apps** like MyFitnessPal provide personalized workout routines and dietary recommendations based on user data.
- **Financial tools** like Plum automate savings by analyzing daily spending patterns.

This personalization isn't just convenient, it's a game-changer.

> A McKinsey study found that businesses leveraging AI for personalization experienced productivity gains of 10–15%. As consumers, we've come to expect these seamless, tailored experiences as part of modern life.

Balancing Personalization and Privacy

However, personalization comes with trade-offs. AI systems rely on vast amounts of personal data, raising concerns about privacy and security. It's crucial to understand how data is collected, stored, and used, and to take steps to protect yourself.

Regulations like the General Data Protection Regulation (GDPR) in the European Union have empowered consumers by enforcing stricter controls on data use. Trust and transparency are critical for the future of AI, and this book will help you navigate these challenges while enjoying the benefits of AI.

How This Book Will Help You

This guide is designed to make AI accessible and actionable for everyone. Whether you want to automate mundane tasks, optimize your finances, enhance your health and wellness, or some help organizing your next trip to Bali, this book will show you how to integrate AI into your life effectively. You don't need a technical background, the content is simple, practical, and tailored to everyday use.

By the end of this journey, you'll not only understand how to use AI to improve your life but also gain insights from specialists into its limitations and ethical considerations. This book will empower you to embrace AI as a trusted partner, enabling a smarter, more efficient, and balanced future.

The possibilities are limitless, and the first step starts here.

What is AI?

Artificial Intelligence (AI) has become an essential part of modern life, enabling machines to mimic human intelligence in ways once thought impossible. Its capabilities—ranging from recognizing patterns to making decisions and learning from experience—continue to revolutionize how we live and work. At its core, AI combines advanced algorithms with adaptive learning models, constantly evolving as it processes new data.

Types of AI

Artificial Intelligence (AI) is categorized based on its capabilities and functions, with each type showcasing unique potential and limitations. These categories are foundational to understanding how AI operates and what it aims to achieve.

Narrow AI (Weak AI)
Narrow AI is the most prevalent form of AI today, designed to excel at specific tasks but incapable of performing beyond its pre-defined scope.

Over 90% of AI applications in use today are Narrow AI systems.

Examples:
- **Voice Assistants:** Siri and Alexa streamline daily tasks such as setting reminders, controlling smart home devices, and answering basic queries.
- **Streaming Platforms**: Netflix uses AI to recommend content by analyzing viewing habits and preferences, offering a personalized entertainment experience.
- **Search Engines**: Google Search processes billions of queries daily, leveraging AI to provide the most relevant and accurate results.
- **Healthcare Applications**: AI systems like IBM Watson analyze medical data to assist in diagnostics, improving efficiency in healthcare services.

Characteristics:
- Focuses exclusively on single, well-defined tasks without the capacity to generalize or adapt to unrelated tasks.
- Operates using supervised learning techniques, requiring labeled datasets to function effectively.
- Examples of Narrow AI systems include image recognition software, spam email filters, and autonomous vehicles operating in controlled environments.

> Narrow AI has proven incredibly effective in customer service. Chatbots powered by AI handle up to 70% of customer interactions for major companies, reducing response times and improving user satisfaction.

General AI (AGI or Strong AI)

General AI represents the hypothetical capability of machines to perform any intellectual task a human can, with reasoning, learning, and problem-solving across multiple disciplines. Unlike Narrow AI, AGI would exhibit adaptability, creativity, and a deeper understanding of the world.

Current Status: AGI remains theoretical, with significant research underway. Advances in unsupervised learning, reinforcement learning, and neural networks have brought us closer but remain far from achieving true AGI.

Characteristics:

- Capable of autonomous learning and problem-solving across diverse domains without human intervention.
- Mimics human cognitive abilities such as abstract reasoning, emotional understanding, and logical thinking.
- Could perform tasks such as writing novels, designing complex engineering solutions, or conducting scientific research without predefined instructions.

> "If AGI becomes a reality, it could fundamentally redefine human-AI collaboration, enabling breakthroughs in science, healthcare, and ethics."
>
> Yoshua Bengio, AI researcher.

Challenges to Development:

- Computational Power: Current hardware cannot support the vast processing requirements needed for AGI.
- Data Understanding: Teaching machines to understand context, intent, and nuance remains a significant hurdle.
- Ethical Concerns: The potential for misuse, job displacement, and loss of human control raises complex societal questions.

> Imagine an AGI system capable of coordinating global disaster relief efforts by analyzing real-time data, allocating resources, and making life-saving decisions, a glimpse into its transformative potential.

Super AI

A speculative concept, Super AI envisions machines surpassing human intelligence in every aspect, including creativity, emotional intelligence, and ethical reasoning. Super AI would not just perform tasks better than humans but could potentially operate autonomously across all areas of life.

Characteristics:
- Beyond human-level reasoning and problem-solving.
- Capable of creating knowledge, innovations, and solutions that humans cannot conceive.
- Could integrate emotional intelligence, creativity, and ethical decision-making into its operations.

> "If AGI becomes a reality, it could fundamentally redefine human-AI collaboration, enabling breakthroughs in science, healthcare, and ethics."
>
> Elon Musk

Speculative Applications and Challenges

Super AI holds the potential to revolutionize industries and solve humanity's most complex problems. For example, it could transform healthcare by designing treatments for previously incurable diseases within hours. In the face of climate change, Super AI's advanced modeling and optimization could develop sustainable solutions that outpace current methods, addressing global environmental challenges with unprecedented precision.

However, these possibilities come with significant challenges and concerns. The most pressing issue is the existential risk, the fear that humans might lose control over such a powerful entity, leading to unpredictable outcomes. Furthermore, there is the question of societal impact: If machines surpass human capabilities in all fields, how would humanity redefine its purpose, role, and meaning in an AI-dominated world?

These discussions highlight the need for careful reflection as we approach the boundaries of AI's capabilities and their implications for the future.

> Isaac Asimov's "Three Laws of Robotics" remain a cornerstone of ethical debates around Super AI, emphasizing safety and human control.

Generative AI

Generative AI is a type of AI that creates new content—text, images, music, code, and even 3D models—based on patterns it learns from data. This category has rapidly gained prominence due to advancements in deep learning models like Transformers.

The AI-generated short film *Sunspring* used GPT to create its script, showcasing the creative potential of Generative AI.

Examples:

- **Text Generation:** OpenAI's GPT models can draft essays, summarize content, or generate code.
- **Image and Video Creation:** DALL·E and Stable Diffusion produce realistic images from textual descriptions.
- **Audio and Music:** Jukedeck and AIVA compose music tailored to specific styles and preferences.
- **DeepFake Technology:** AI-powered tools can synthesize realistic videos, sparking debates about their ethical implications.

Applications:

- **Healthcare:** Generative AI designs molecular structures for drug discovery.
- **Entertainment:** AI-generated art and movies, such as *Sunspring*, push creative boundaries.
- **Education:** Automated generation of personalized learning materials.

> By 2024, generative AI is expected to contribute more than $50 billion to the global economy through innovations in media, entertainment, and healthcare.

Evolutionary AI (Emerging Concept)

Evolutionary AI uses algorithms inspired by natural selection to solve problems, constantly evolving to find optimal solutions. This category is particularly effective in complex environments requiring continuous adaptation.

Applications:
- **Robotics:** Designing movement strategies for robots to navigate challenging terrains.
- **Engineering:** Optimizing supply chain logistics or energy systems for greater efficiency.

Characteristics:
- Simulates biological evolution to refine itself over time.
- Adapts dynamically to changing environments.

> Evolutionary AI represents a shift from rule-based learning to models that dynamically adapt and grow over time, mirroring natural selection.

Functional Categories of AI

AI can also be classified based on its functional capabilities, showcasing its progression toward greater sophistication:

Reactive AI refers to simple systems that respond to inputs without the ability to store memory or learn from past experiences. These systems are highly specialized, performing pre-defined tasks with precision. A well-known example is Deep Blue, IBM's chess-playing computer, which famously defeated a world chess champion in 1997 by analyzing moves and predicting outcomes in real time.

Limited Memory AI encompasses most modern AI systems, which are capable of learning from data and improving their performance over time. These systems rely on historical information to make decisions, such as self-driving cars that analyze traffic patterns, obstacles, and past driving data to navigate safely.

Theory of Mind AI represents a future stage in AI development, where systems will possess the ability to understand human emotions, intentions, and thought processes. This form of AI aims to interact more intuitively with humans by recognizing non-verbal cues, fostering deeper collaboration, and anticipating needs. Though still in the conceptual phase, it marks a significant leap in human-AI interaction.

Self-Aware AI remains speculative, representing a hypothetical form of artificial intelligence that would possess consciousness and self-awareness. Such systems would not only understand their existence but also have the ability to reflect, make autonomous decisions, and potentially experience emotions. While the concept raises exciting possibilities, it also prompts critical ethical and philosophical discussions about the role of AI in society and its implications for humanity.

Understanding these categories highlights how AI systems evolve from reactive tools to potential collaborators with emotional and cognitive depth, sparking curiosity and careful consideration as we move forward.

> "Artificial Intelligence will either be the best or worst thing to happen to humanity"
>
> Stephen Hawking

A Historical Overview

Alan Turing's groundbreaking ideas about machines exhibiting human-like intelligence, introduced in his seminal 1950 paper *"Computing Machinery and Intelligence,"* sparked a wide range of reactions, from fascination to skepticism. In this paper, Turing posed the provocative question, "Can machines think?" and proposed the Turing Test as a way to assess whether a machine could exhibit behavior indistinguishable from that of a human. While revolutionary, his ideas ignited both philosophical debates and practical concerns.

Among academics and researchers, Turing's theories were met with considerable intellectual curiosity and excitement. His concept of a "universal machine," now known as the Turing Machine, had already transformed the way computation was understood, laying the groundwork for modern computer science. Many saw his ideas as a pathway to automating labor-intensive tasks and solving complex problems, inspiring a generation of scientists to explore the possibilities of artificial intelligence. His work directly influenced the 1956 Dartmouth Conference, which formally established AI as a field of study.

However, skepticism and criticism were equally prominent. At the time, computing technology was still in its infancy, and many doubted whether machines could realistically mimic human thought. Practical limitations made even simple computational tasks arduous and resource-intensive. Philosophers, too, raised objections, with figures like John Searle later arguing that machines could only simulate thinking but never truly achieve consciousness or understanding. This philosophical skepticism sparked enduring debates on the nature of intelligence and the mind-body problem. Meanwhile, societal fears about technology, often fueled by science fiction, led some to worry about the potential dangers of intelligent machines. The notion that machines might one day surpass human control seemed both thrilling and terrifying.

For the broader public, Turing's work was largely inaccessible at the time, as AI remained a niche academic pursuit. Yet the concept of "thinking machines" began to permeate popular culture, particularly through science fiction, which alternately depicted intelligent machines as humanity's saviors or existential threats. This dual narrative of fascination and fear continues to influence perceptions of AI today.

Despite initial skepticism and the technological limitations of his era, Turing's ideas laid the intellectual foundation for decades of advancements in computing and artificial intelligence. The Turing Test remains a fundamental benchmark for assessing machine intelligence, while his broader theories have shaped the philosophical and practical exploration of AI. Over time, Turing has come to be celebrated as a visionary thinker who was far ahead of his time, his legacy underscoring the profound impact of his work on our understanding of intelligence, machines, and the potential of human ingenuity.

Alan Turing's pioneering work laid the groundwork for machine intelligence, sparking debates and research that shaped the future of AI. His vision of "thinking" machines was revolutionary, though its realization was complex and gradual. From the coining of "artificial intelligence" to breakthroughs in deep learning, AI's evolution reflects a journey of discovery, setbacks, and triumphs. Each milestone builds on Turing's ideas, driving the creation of machines that learn, reason, and assist humanity. Let's explore the key moments that transformed AI into a cornerstone of modern innovation.

1950s: Laying the Groundwork

- **1950:** Alan Turing published *"Computing Machinery and Intelligence"*, posing the question, "Can machines think?" He also proposed the Turing Test to evaluate a machine's ability to exhibit human-like intelligence.

- **1956:** The term *"artificial intelligence"* was coined by John McCarthy at the Dartmouth Conference, which formally established AI as a discipline and brought together pioneers like Marvin Minsky and Herbert Simon.

1960s: Early Triumphs in Symbolic AI

- **1965:** Joseph Weizenbaum developed *ELIZA*, one of the first chatbots capable of mimicking human conversation using natural language processing.

- **1966:** *Shakey the Robot* was introduced as the first robot to navigate its surroundings autonomously, combining sensors and logic.

1970s: Challenges and Revival

- **1970:** The expert system *DENDRAL* was created to help chemists analyze molecular structures, proving AI's potential in specialized fields.

- **1972:** The programming language *PROLOG* was developed, becoming a key tool for AI research.

- **1974–1980:** The "AI Winter" marked a period of stagnation due to overhyped expectations, technical limitations, and reduced funding.

- **Late 1970s:** *Expert systems* like MYCIN demonstrated practical applications of AI in fields such as healthcare.

1980s: The Resurgence of AI

- **1986:** Geoffrey Hinton and colleagues introduced the backpropagation algorithm, enabling the training of deep neural networks and reigniting interest in AI.

- **1987–1993:** A second "AI Winter" occurred as inflated expectations again outpaced real-world capabilities.

- **1980s:** AI systems became widely adopted in business for tasks like inventory management and financial forecasting.

1990s: Breakthroughs in Intelligence

- **1997:** IBM's *Deep Blue* defeated chess grandmaster Garry Kasparov, highlighting AI's ability to handle complex strategic problems.

- **1990s:** Programs like *Dragon Dictate* advanced speech recognition technology, paving the way for modern voice assistants.

2000s: Data-Driven Progress

- **2004:** The *DARPA Grand Challenge* spurred innovation in autonomous vehicle technology, with self-driving cars navigating real-world terrains.

- **2009:** Google launched its self-driving car project, solidifying AI's potential in transportation.

- **Late 2000s:** The explosion of big data enabled AI to analyze massive datasets, driving advancements in targeted advertising and personalized recommendations.

2010s: The Deep Learning Revolution

- **2012:** Neural networks achieved groundbreaking results in image and speech recognition, largely thanks to advancements in deep learning techniques.

- **2014:** Chatbot *Eugene Goostman* became the first AI to "pass" the Turing Test, convincing judges it was a human.

- **2016:** Google DeepMind's *AlphaGo* defeated world champion Lee Sedol in the game of Go, showcasing the power of reinforcement learning.

- **2017:** Google introduced *Transformer models*, leading to transformative advancements in natural language processing (NLP). This eventually enabled systems like GPT and BERT.

2020s: AI in Everyday Life

- **2021:** OpenAI's *GPT-3* and *DALL·E* showcased the potential of generative AI in creating human-like text and images.

- **2022:** AI models like ChatGPT and Stable Diffusion brought generative AI to the mainstream, transforming industries such as content creation, education, and customer service.

- **Present Day:** AI is integrated into daily life through virtual assistants, self-driving vehicles, personalized recommendations, and ethical AI discussions focusing on transparency, bias, and accountability.

"As AI transitioned from theory to practical application, each milestone reflected our collective drive to expand the boundaries of intelligence, solving problems we once thought unsolvable."

AI's *Aha* Moments

Over the decades, artificial intelligence has moved from a niche concept in research labs to a transformative force in everyday life, punctuated by key "aha" moments that made its potential undeniable to the general public. These milestones didn't just demonstrate the capabilities of AI; they captured imaginations, sparked debates, and revealed how deeply AI was beginning to shape the world.

One of the first watershed moments was **IBM's Deep Blue defeating chess grandmaster Garry Kasparov in 1997**. This event shocked audiences worldwide as a machine triumphed in a game long seen as the pinnacle of human strategic thinking. Deep Blue's victory wasn't just about winning a chess match—it was a tangible demonstration of how machines could outperform humans in tasks requiring advanced planning and foresight.

Years later, Google DeepMind's AlphaGo achieved a similar leap forward, but on an even more complex playing field. **In 2016, AlphaGo defeated world champion Lee Sedol in the game of Go**, a strategy game with infinitely more possible moves than chess. The victory revealed the sophistication of modern AI, showcasing its ability to learn and adapt using deep reinforcement learning. For many, it was a wake-up call: AI wasn't just executing pre-programmed strategies; it was teaching itself how to win.

While games captured headlines, another "aha" moment unfolded quietly in people's pockets. **The rise of voice assistants like Siri, Alexa, and Google Assistant** brought AI into daily routines, making it conversational, relatable, and indispensable. Suddenly, people could speak to their devices to check the weather, manage calendars, and control their homes. These tools transformed AI from an abstract idea into something millions interacted with effortlessly, often without even realizing they were using AI.

Then came a revolution that literally hit the streets: autonomous driving. **Tesla's introduction of Autopilot in 2015** and its subsequent Full Self-Driving (FSD) features turned the idea of self-driving cars from science fiction into reality. Videos of Teslas changing lanes, navigating highways, and parking themselves went viral, capturing the public's imagination. Unlike AI behind screens or in games, autonomous driving was a visible, tangible application of AI in action, navigating real-world complexities in real time. Companies like Waymo further pushed boundaries by rolling out fully autonomous taxis, making people realize that AI wasn't just assisting, it was taking over tasks long considered uniquely human.

But the latest and perhaps most groundbreaking "aha" moment came with the rise of generative AI, embodied by tools like **ChatGPT, DALL·E,** and other advanced models. Introduced to the mainstream in late 2022, ChatGPT stunned the public with its ability to generate human-like text, answer questions, write essays, and even engage in creative storytelling—all with remarkable fluency and coherence. What made this moment different was its accessibility: millions of people could interact directly with an AI capable of creating content that felt truly intelligent and creative. Whether writing code, drafting emails, or brainstorming ideas, tools like ChatGPT showcased AI's ability to assist in ways that felt personal and immediate.

Generative AI didn't stop at text. Platforms like DALL·E and MidJourney pushed the boundaries of visual creativity by generating artwork from simple text descriptions. Suddenly, anyone could create professional-quality visuals without needing artistic skills. For many, these tools felt like magic, demonstrating that AI wasn't just about analyzing data or performing logical tasks, it was stepping into the realms of creativity and imagination.

These milestones collectively reshaped public perception of AI, proving its transformative power across vastly different domains—from intellectual strategy to practical convenience, real-world navigation, and now, creative collaboration. Each breakthrough brought AI closer to the forefront of daily life, erasing the boundary between what was once thought impossible and what has become routine.

The culmination of these moments not only demonstrated AI's capabilities but also fueled questions about its future. If AI could outthink chess and Go champions, hold conversations, safely navigate our streets, and create art and literature, what else could it achieve? Generative AI's arrival marked a new chapter in this journey, turning AI into not just a tool but a creative partner, opening up possibilities we are only beginning to explore.

AI is not just a tool for the future, it is the key to unlocking smarter, more efficient living today.

Practical AI in Daily Life

In today's fast-paced world, people face a variety of challenges, whether it's managing a demanding schedule, striving for personal growth, or balancing family life with professional ambitions. For the shy individual trying to build confidence in social situations, the busy parent juggling work and home responsibilities, or the aspiring professional seeking to stand out in their career, AI can provide valuable support.

Imagine the shy person who wants to improve their communication skills. AI-powered tools, such as language apps or virtual communication coaches, can simulate real-world interactions, helping them practice and gain confidence without fear of judgment. For the over-scheduled parent with kids, pets, and a to-do list a mile long, AI assistants like Alexa or Google Assistant can automate daily tasks like, setting reminders, creating grocery lists, and even scheduling family activities to reclaim precious time.

For professionals aiming to advance their careers, AI can act as a career coach, helping them polish their resumes, practice for interviews with feedback-driven tools, or even identify skill gaps through platforms like LinkedIn Learning. Meanwhile, for those with fitness goals, AI can serve as a personal trainer, delivering customized workout plans, tracking progress, and providing encouragement along the way.

AI isn't just about meeting goals, it's also about setting boundaries and creating habits to protect mental and emotional well-being. For someone struggling to say no to excessive work demands, AI productivity tools can flag when they're overcommitting and suggest healthier schedules. Habit-tracking apps, enhanced by AI, help users stick to new routines, like daily meditation or journaling, offering gentle nudges and insights along the journey.

It's important to note that while AI isn't a magic solution for every challenge, it can be a powerful ally. Different people, with unique goals and obstacles, can use AI as a tool to ease their journey and improve their quality of life. Whether it's about enhancing productivity, finding balance, or reaching personal milestones, AI offers accessible, practical ways to make progress in areas that matter most.

Ultimately, for anyone looking for something new—be it better organization, personal growth, or even just more free time—AI can make a meaningful difference. It's not about replacing effort or determination but amplifying what's already within us to achieve more with less stress.

Let's explore practical ways AI can transform your everyday life.

Managing Daily Tasks

Balancing daily responsibilities can feel overwhelming, especially when modern lifestyles demand so much of our time and energy. For households where both parents work full-time, the pressures of maintaining professional success and a nurturing home environment can be immense. Add societal expectations from social media, the pursuit of a "perfect" life, and it's no surprise that essential but routine tasks like grocery shopping, scheduling appointments, and managing household chores often feel daunting.

AI is stepping in to lighten the load. By automating routine tasks, AI tools allow individuals to prioritize what truly matters. For instance, grocery apps track supplies and suggest shopping lists, smart assistants schedule meetings or remind you of deadlines, and home automation systems manage lighting, security, and even thermostat settings. These technologies reduce the mental burden of task management, freeing up time for family, hobbies, or simply a moment to unwind.

Practical Use:
Pedro, a busy entrepreneur, relies on Google Assistant to juggle multiple responsibilities. By saying, "Hey Google, schedule a meeting tomorrow at 2 PM" or "Remind me to pick up dry cleaning at 5 PM," he automates reminders that sync across all his devices.

> Amazon Alexa processed over 1 billion voice commands in 2023, demonstrating the growing reliance on virtual assistants.
>
> Source: Amazon AI Report

Virtual Assistants

Virtual assistants such as Google Assistant, Amazon Alexa, and Apple Siri have revolutionized how we interact with technology. They understand and respond to voice commands, making it effortless to organize tasks, control smart devices, and search for information. By creating seamless connections between users and their devices, virtual assistants save time and simplify life.

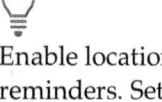

Enable location-based reminders. Set "Remind me to buy bread when I'm near the grocery store" avoiding forgetting.

Practical Use:

Tom returns home to find the perfect ambiance, thanks to his Google Nest thermostat and Philips Hue lighting, which are both controlled by his virtual assistant, creating a seamless and welcoming experience..

Grocery Shopping and Lists

Grocery shopping can be effortless with AI. Apps like AnyList, Out of Milk, and Alexa track items and even suggest purchases based on past shopping habits. Advanced smart refrigerators like Samsung Family Hub take this further by monitoring inventory and expiration dates.

Link your grocery app to delivery services like Instacart. Simply select items from your AI-synced list and have them delivered to you.

Practical Use:

Sarah, a mother of three, finds Alexa indispensable. When she runs out of eggs while cooking, she says, "Alexa, add eggs to the shopping list." At the store, her Alexa app displays an updated list, ensuring no item is forgotten.

> Smart refrigerators reduce food waste by up to 40%, saving households approximately $1,500 annually.
> Source: FoodTec Insights

Smart Home Automation

AI-powered devices like Nest thermostats, Ring cameras, and Philips Hue lighting systems transform home management by learning user preferences and automating routine tasks..

Schedule routines using AI assistants, such as "Goodnight mode" to turn off lights, lock doors, and lower the thermostat with a single command.

Practical Use:

Vera uses her Ring Doorbell to monitor her home's security while at work. Meanwhile, her smart thermostat adjusts the temperature automatically based on her habits, ensuring comfort and energy efficiency.

> Studies show that smart thermostats can reduce energy consumption by up to 20%, making homes eco-friendly and cost-effective
> Source: Greentech Research

Finance and Budgeting

Managing money becomes significantly easier with AI, as tools analyze spending, provide personalized insights, and automate investments. In today's rapidly changing world, financial security is more important than ever. The way we approach our finances determines not just our immediate stability but also the opportunities we create for ourselves in the future.

AI empowers individuals to take control of their financial well-being by offering deeper clarity and actionable insights. It allows us to identify patterns in spending, understand where our money goes, and uncover areas where we might be overspending. With this newfound awareness, managing budgets becomes less of a chore and more of an opportunity to align financial habits with long-term goals.

Financial literacy is no longer a skill reserved for experts or professionals. It's a necessity for anyone who wishes to feel secure in their choices, whether it's saving for unexpected events, planning for retirement, or ensuring financial independence. AI doesn't just simplify processes; it helps people start thinking strategically about their financial health. It encourages reflection on questions like, "Am I prepared for the future Am I using my resources wisely? Could I be doing more to safeguard my financial stability?" By leveraging AI, we can shift our focus from short-term decision-making to a more holistic view of personal and family finances.

Budgeting Tools

Apps like Mint, PocketGuard, and YNAB help users monitor spending, categorize expenses, and create actionable plans for saving money.

Practical Use:

Julia links her bank accounts to Mint, which categorizes her transactions into dining, groceries, and entertainment. Weekly reports highlight her spending trends, allowing her to identify areas to cut back.

Use AI alerts to notify you of unusual transactions or when you're nearing your budget limit in a category.

Budgeting apps powered by AI saved users an average of $5,000 annually in 2022 through smarter spending recommendations.

Source: FinTech Report

Automated Investments

AI-powered platforms like Betterment and Wealthfront manage investments by analyzing market trends and automatically rebalancing portfolios. These tools provide a hands-off approach to wealth building, ensuring your investments stay aligned with your financial goals

 Set up recurring contributions to your AI-managed investment account. Even $100 a month can grow to significantly over time.

Practical Use:

John, an engineer, uses Betterment to grow his savings. The AI tailors his portfolio based on his goals, such as buying a house in 10 years, and adjusts it according to market changes.

> Robo-advisors managed over $2 trillion in assets globally by 2023, democratizing access to financial advice.
>
> Source: PwC Report

Health and Fitness

AI tools are revolutionizing the way we approach personal health, offering unprecedented opportunities to take control of our well-being. In today's health-conscious world, where staying fit, eating well, and maintaining mental wellness have become essential pillars of modern living, the integration of AI into personal health management is a game-changer. These tools don't just track our habits—they empower us with actionable insights that make it easier to make informed decisions about fitness, nutrition, and overall wellness.

Every day, new discoveries and studies emerge, shedding light on what it means to lead a healthy and active life. From breakthroughs in understanding the role of gut health in immunity to the benefits of interval training for cardiovascular health, the sheer volume of information can be overwhelming. AI bridges the gap between scientific advancements and everyday application. It distills complex data into simple, personalized recommendations that are easy to incorporate into our daily routines. By analyzing our unique patterns, preferences, and goals, AI turns abstract knowledge into tangible actions.

For fitness, AI tools provide tailored workout plans that evolve with our progress. They consider factors such as our fitness level, goals, and even how much time we have available. Whether it's a smartwatch reminding us to stand and stretch or an AI-powered app suggesting a mix of cardio and strength training based on our energy levels, these tools help us integrate physical activity seamlessly into busy schedules. For those who find exercise intimidating or lack the time for traditional routines, AI makes fitness approachable, guiding users step-by-step and celebrating small victories that build momentum.

When it comes to nutrition, AI takes guesswork out of eating well. Apps powered by AI can analyze dietary habits and suggest meal plans that align with health goals, whether it's weight management, muscle building, or simply feeling more energetic. By scanning grocery receipts or tracking food logs, AI identifies nutrient deficiencies and offers solutions tailored to individual tastes and lifestyles. It can even provide real-time feedback, like flagging high sugar intake or recommending hydration after a rigorous workout, helping us stay accountable in real-time.

Wellness, often overlooked in traditional health approaches, also benefits immensely from AI. Tools that monitor sleep patterns provide insights into how we can improve rest and recovery. Mental health apps leverage AI to offer mindfulness exercises, stress management techniques, and even emotional check-ins, fostering a holistic view of health. By integrating these tools into our lives, AI not only supports physical fitness but also nurtures mental resilience, which is equally critical in today's fast-paced world.

The most significant advantage of AI-driven health tools is accessibility. They bring the expertise of a personal trainer, nutritionist, and wellness coach into the palm of our hands, democratizing access to information and resources that were once exclusive or expensive. Whether we're trying to manage a chronic condition, improve athletic performance, or simply lead a more balanced life, AI equips us with the knowledge and guidance to make meaningful changes.

Ultimately, the responsibility to be healthier and more active lies with us. AI provides the tools and insights, but we must take the steps. It's not about achieving perfection but about making small, consistent choices that add up over time. With the support of AI, we can break down the barriers that hold us back, whether it's lack of time, knowledge, or motivation, and transform our aspirations for better health into a sustainable lifestyle. In this way, AI not only enhances our ability to care for ourselves but also empowers us to take ownership of our health journey, ensuring we live our best, most active lives.

Fitness Trackers

Wearables like Fitbit, Apple Watch, and WHOOP monitor metrics such as activity levels, sleep quality, and heart rate.

Use your fitness tracker's AI to set daily movement goals and enable reminders for long periods of inactivity.

Practical Use:

Lisa uses her Apple Watch to track her steps and sleep patterns. The AI suggests improvements, like going to bed earlier to achieve better REM sleep, based on her weekly trends.

Fitness AI users achieved a 30% higher adherence rate to workout routines compared to traditional methods.

Source: Journal of Health AI

Workout Recommendations

Apps like Freeletics and MyFitnessPal offer personalized workout routines based on individual goals, fitness levels, and progress.

These tools provide motivation through real-time feedback, making it easier to stay consistent and track improvements over time.

Practical Use:
Leandro, a fitness newbie, follows Freeletics' AI-generated plan. As he gains strength, the app increases intensity, ensuring consistent improvement without burnout

Pet Care

AI is transforming the way pet owners care for their furry companions, offering solutions that bring convenience, peace of mind, and, ultimately, a stronger bond between humans and their pets. In our fast-paced lives, where time is often a luxury, managing daily responsibilities can feel overwhelming. As a result, trivial yet necessary tasks like feeding, exercising, and monitoring the health of pets may be overlooked, contributing to stress and sometimes leading to heartbreaking decisions, such as rehoming or surrendering animals. However, AI-powered tools and technologies are emerging as a lifeline for pet owners, making it easier to meet the demands of pet care while balancing the complexities of modern life.

One of the primary challenges pet owners face is ensuring their pets' needs are met consistently, even when life gets busy. Whether it's long work hours, weekend getaways, or unforeseen events, the pressure to maintain a routine can be daunting. AI tools, such as automated feeders and health trackers, step in to fill this gap by providing seamless solutions that cater to a pet's needs around the clock. These devices not only ensure that pets are fed on time and in the right portions but also keep track of their health metrics, alerting owners to potential issues before they escalate. For example, a smart collar can monitor activity levels, sleep patterns, and even unusual behavior, acting as an early warning system for illnesses. This proactive approach to pet care can prevent minor health concerns from becoming serious problems, reducing the emotional and financial strain on pet owners.

For those who struggle with time constraints, AI tools offer unparalleled convenience. Imagine a busy professional who spends hours commuting or a parent juggling family responsibilities. In such scenarios, automated devices like self-cleaning litter boxes and AI-enabled toys can save valuable time while ensuring pets remain happy and comfortable. These technologies eliminate the need for constant supervision, allowing owners to focus on other responsibilities without feeling guilty about neglecting their furry friends. Additionally, AI solutions like pet cameras with treat dispensers enable remote interaction, ensuring that pets feel loved and engaged even when their humans are away. This level of connectivity can be a game-changer for owners who travel frequently or work long hours, as it bridges the gap between physical absence and emotional presence.

Vacations and weekend getaways, which often pose logistical challenges for pet owners, are another area where AI shines. Many people hesitate to travel or feel compelled to give up their pets due to the perceived difficulty of ensuring their care during absences. AI-powered boarding systems and apps that connect owners with reliable pet sitters simplify this process, offering real-time updates and peace of mind. Smart feeders and water dispensers can also minimize reliance on external help, enabling pets to maintain their routine with minimal disruption. These tools empower owners to enjoy their time away without constant worry, fostering a healthier relationship with their pets upon return.

The stress of managing a pet's health, particularly for individuals with limited experience or knowledge, can also lead to feelings of inadequacy and, in some cases, surrendering animals. AI is changing this narrative by democratizing access to professional-grade insights and guidance. Apps that analyze dietary needs, suggest exercise routines, and provide training tips make it easier for owners to feel confident in their ability to care for their pets. Moreover, AI helps streamline veterinary care by enabling remote consultations, digital health records, and even early diagnosis through data analysis. By making pet health more accessible and manageable, AI reduces the likelihood of preventable diseases and injuries, ensuring that pets live longer, happier lives.

Ultimately, the integration of AI into pet care goes beyond convenience; it addresses some of the core reasons why pet owners struggle to meet their responsibilities. By reducing the time and effort required for daily tasks, AI empowers people to focus on the joy of pet ownership rather than the challenges. It fosters stronger bonds between pets and their owners, reduces the rate of pet abandonment, and encourages a more responsible and sustainable approach to pet care. In this way, AI not only revolutionizes how we manage our furry companions but also strengthens the emotional connection that makes pets an irreplaceable part of our lives.

Automated Feeding Systems

AI feeders like PetSafe Smart Feed ensure precise meal portions for pets, while Litter-Robot 4 simplifies litter box maintenance for cat owners.

Use activity-tracking collars like Fi Smart Collar to monitor your dog's exercise levels and health metrics.

Practical Use:

Maria uses PetSafe to feed her dog Max at scheduled times, even when she's at work. Notifications ensure she never forgets to refill the food tray. And Clara's Litter-Robot automatically cleans Luna's litter box and notifies her when the waste drawer is full, keeping her home odor-free without daily scooping.

AI-powered pet gadgets saved pet owners an average of 6 hours per week on feeding, cleaning, and exercise tracking.
Source: PetTech Review

Pet Cameras and Monitors

Devices like Furbo Dog Camera allow owners to check on pets remotely and dispense treats while providing bark and motion alerts. These features offer peace of mind, ensuring pets are safe and entertained even when their owners are away

Practical Use:
Diana uses Furbo to monitor Bella when at work. If Bella barks excessively, Diana speaks to her through the camera and rewards her with a treat to calm her down.

Health Monitoring Devices
AI-powered devices like Fi Smart Collar track activity, sleep, and health metrics, while Whistle Health alerts owners to changes in pet behavior. These tools help detect potential health issues early, ensuring pets receive timely care and attention.

Practical Use:
Francis noticed Max's reduced activity through the Whistle app and consulted a vet early, identifying and addressing a joint issue before it worsened.

Travelling

Like I've been saying a lot during this book, we do live in a fast-paced environment where the demands of work, family, and everyday life leave little room to breathe. Taking time for a vacation is no longer just a luxury; it's a vital part of maintaining our mental, physical, and emotional health. Yet, even the idea of planning a getaway can feel daunting, especially in an age where social media constantly bombards us with endless destination ideas, picture-perfect itineraries, and "must-visit" spots. With so many options, it's easy to feel overwhelmed or unsure about where to start.

This is where AI is stepping in to transform the travel and tourism experience, making it seamless, personalized, and deeply enriching. AI-powered tools simplify every step of the journey, from curating the perfect itinerary to offering real-time navigation in unfamiliar destinations. Platforms like Google Travel and Hopper predict airfare trends, helping travelers save money and make confident decisions. Personalized AI recommendations ensure that trips are tailored to individual preferences, eliminating the stress of planning and allowing people to focus on what truly matters: enjoying the experience.

But here's an important reminder: vacations should be about more than ticking off bucket-list destinations or sharing picture-perfect moments on social media. While social media can inspire wanderlust, it can also create unnecessary pressure to craft a journey that looks good for others rather than feels good for ourselves. I encourage everyone to step away from the constant need to document and showcase every moment—unless, of course, this is your job—and focus instead on being present.

Allow yourself to truly feel the moments you've planned for, whether that's marveling at a breathtaking sunset, savoring local cuisine, or simply relaxing without distractions. AI can take care of the logistics, but it's up to you to embrace the experience fully. By using AI to ease the practicalities of travel, you're free to prioritize what really matters: recharging your mind, body, and spirit in a way that's meaningful to you. After all, a vacation should be about you—not about meeting anyone else's expectations.

Automated Travel Planning

Platforms like Google Travel and Skyscanner use AI to curate personalized itineraries and provide dynamic pricing insights. These tools help travelers find the best deals and create trips tailored to their preferences.

Always download offline versions of AI maps and translation apps before traveling to areas with limited connectivity

Practical Use:

Sophia, a digital nomad, uses the AI-powered app Hopper to plan her travels. The app predicts airfare trends and sends alerts for the best booking times, helping Sophia save money and reduce stress. Hopper's AI technology analyzes over a billion flight prices daily to recommend the perfect time to book.

Navigation and Language Translation

AI tools ensure travelers can navigate unfamiliar locations effortlessly. GPS systems like Google Maps provide real-time traffic updates, while translation tools break down language barriers.

Practical Use:

While exploring Tokyo, Marco uses Google Lens to translate Japanese signs and menus in real time. This makes his trip more immersive and enjoyable as he understands his surroundings better.

> AI-based translation apps now support over 100 languages, making international travel more accessible than ever.
>
> Source: Google Translate

Smart Transportation

AI enhances transportation with innovations like autonomous vehicles and efficient public transport systems. At smart airports, AI streamlines check-ins with facial recognition, while ride-sharing platforms optimize matching drivers with passengers.

Use ride-sharing apps during peak times to save on fares as AI matches multiple passengers traveling similar routes.

Practical Use:

At Singapore's Changi Airport, Emma uses facial recognition for check-in and boarding, bypassing traditional boarding passes and speeding up her journey.

> AI-driven smart airports reduce wait times by up to 30%, improving overall passenger satisfaction.
> Source: The International Air Transport Association (IATA)

Immersive Travel with AI

AI-powered augmented reality (AR) apps provide interactive travel experiences. Tourists can explore historical sites with overlays of detailed information, adding depth to their adventures.

Practical Use:

While visiting the Colosseum in Rome, Ahmed uses an AR app to visualize how the amphitheater appeared in its prime. The AI-powered guide brings history to life, making Ahmed's experience unforgettable.

Artificial Intelligence enhances every aspect of daily life, from scheduling errands to managing health and finances. With AI as a dependable ally, individuals can optimize their routines, make informed decisions, and enjoy greater convenience. As these technologies evolve, their potential to further personalize and enrich our lives grows, offering endless possibilities. In the next chapter, we'll explore how AI empowers professional productivity and career growth.

Jobs & Workplace

Artificial intelligence is revolutionizing not only how people search for jobs but also how they perform their roles in the workplace. The daily grind, often consuming more hours than we spend with our families or on personal well-being, is being transformed. AI is stepping in to take over repetitive and time-consuming tasks, allowing us to focus on more meaningful work and even potentially reclaim some of our time for ourselves.

This isn't an entirely new concept. Over the years, manual tasks have gradually been replaced by machines to increase efficiency and reduce labor-intensive work. For instance, in the early industrial era, assembly lines revolutionized manufacturing, replacing repetitive human tasks with mechanical precision. Later, computers automated data processing, transforming industries such as banking and accounting. Now, AI is taking this evolution to the next level by automating not just physical labor but also cognitive tasks. Think of how AI can now write reports, organize meetings, analyze data, or even create presentations.

However, this transformation is happening at an unprecedented pace. A study conducted by OpenAI concluded that 80% of workers in the U.S. could see at least 10% of their tasks automated in the near future. Similarly, a report published by Goldman Sachs in March 2023 predicted that 300 million jobs worldwide would be impacted by AI. While the fear of job losses is natural, the report also highlighted a silver lining: AI adoption could significantly boost team productivity. Rather than replacing workers, AI has the potential to empower them, enabling more focused, strategic, and creative work.

The integration of AI into the workplace is more than a trend; it's a fundamental shift in how we approach work itself. Personalized job recommendation platforms save job seekers countless hours by matching them with opportunities tailored to their skills and experience. In offices, AI tools simplify complex processes, such as transcribing meetings into actionable summaries, scheduling appointments, and managing project timelines. These efficiencies mean fewer hours spent on administrative tasks, freeing up time for creativity, strategic thinking, or simply stepping away from the desk.

Imagine a future where the average workweek shrinks because AI handles many of the routine tasks that currently consume our days. Instead of spending long hours at a desk, we could dedicate more time to personal development, family, hobbies, or other pursuits that enrich our lives. This isn't just wishful thinking. Countries experimenting with shorter workweeks, like the four-day workweek trials in Iceland and New Zealand, have shown that productivity doesn't necessarily decline when people work fewer hours. AI could be the enabler that makes this possible on a global scale.

Of course, this shift requires us to embrace AI thoughtfully. It's about using the power of AI to complement our work rather than seeing it as a threat. Instead of fearing job loss, we can upskill ourselves to work alongside AI, focusing on uniquely human traits such as empathy, creativity, and complex problem-solving—skills that machines cannot replicate. The goal is to **leverage AI to work smarter, not harder.**

The question isn't whether AI will reshape the way we work, it already is. The opportunity lies in how we adapt, grow, and use this transformation to redefine productivity and reclaim time for the things that matter most.

Job Search

AI-powered platforms like LinkedIn, Indeed, and Glassdoor are revolutionizing how people find jobs by personalizing recommendations and simplifying the application process. These tools save time and increase the chances of finding a role that aligns with career goals.

Use tools like Interview Warmup by Google to practice and refine interview responses with real-time feedback.

Practical Use:

David relies on LinkedIn's AI-driven recommendations to match him with job opportunities that align with his experience and skills.

> AI job-matching tools have reduced the average job search time by 25%
>
> Source: CareerTech Insights

Meeting Management

AI tools like Otter.ai, AI Minutes by Avoma, and Fireflies.ai are transforming how meetings are managed by automating tasks like transcription, summarization, and note-taking.

Practical Use:

Sarah uses Otter.ai to transcribe team meetings. After the meeting, the tool generates actionable summaries and organizes deadlines, ensuring that her team stays aligned. By automating these tasks, Sarah saves hours of manual work every week.

Integrate Otter.ai with Zoom or Microsoft Teams for real-time transcription during virtual meetings.

Workflow Automation

AI-powered platforms like Zapier, Asana AI, and Trello AI automate repetitive tasks, such as data entry, task allocation, and performance tracking, improving productivity and reducing stress.

Practical Use:

Carlos's team uses Asana AI to assign tasks and monitor progress. The AI recommends optimal deadlines and identifies bottlenecks, ensuring projects stay on track and meet deadlines efficiently.

Use Zapier to connect multiple tools and automate workflows across different platforms effortlessly.

Workflow automation has been shown to increase team productivity by 20%

Source: Productivity Trends Research

Creative Productivity

AI tools like ChatGPT, Co-pilot, and DALL.E are revolutionizing content creation, coding, and visual design, enabling faster and more creative outputs.

Practical Use:

John, a freelance graphic designer, uses DALL.E to generate unique visual concepts for his clients. This allows him to produce designs more efficiently and explore ideas that wouldn't have been possible manually.

Use ChatGPT to draft email templates, create meeting minutes, or brainstorm ideas to save time and energy.

Recruitment

AI platforms like HireVue, Greenhouse, and LinkedIn Recruiter streamline the recruitment process, from screening resumes to assessing candidates during interviews. By automating these steps, recruiters can focus on finding the best fit while reducing time-to-hire and improving candidate experience.

Practical Use:

A recruiter at a tech company uses HireVue's AI to screen applicants. The system ranks candidates based on their alignment with job requirements, saving hours of manual review and ensuring an unbiased selection process.

> Companies using AI in recruitment fill roles 30% faster on average
>
> Source: HR Insights

Professional Development

Platforms like Coursera, edX, and LinkedIn Learning use AI to recommend courses and build personalized learning paths, helping professionals advance in their careers. These platforms also track progress and suggest skills in high demand, ensuring users stay competitive in a rapidly changing job market.

Practical Use:

Nina wanted to improve her data analysis skills. Using LinkedIn Learning, she received a customized learning path based on her current expertise and career goals, which ultimately helped her secure a promotion.

In the near future, AI might become the catalyst for reimagining what work-life balance truly means. By automating routine tasks and allowing us to concentrate on high-value activities, AI gives us the opportunity to redefine productivity and success, not in terms of hours worked but in terms of meaningful contributions and personal fulfillment.

Making Smart Choices

In this chapter, we've looked at a variety of tools, gadgets, and devices that use AI to make everyday life easier and better. And while these innovations are exciting, we want to emphasize something important: there's no need to feel pressured into buying every shiny gadget or app that comes along. AI is advancing rapidly, and every day, new features and products hit the market. But that doesn't mean you have to keep up with every trend.

The key is to focus on *what's truly important to you*. Identify the areas in your life where you feel AI can genuinely add value, whether it's managing your time better, improving your health, caring for your pets, or simplifying household tasks. Once you've pinpointed your priorities, you can decide where it makes sense to make an investment.

We also encourage you to look for free or low-cost alternatives as a starting point. Many AI-powered tools offer free versions or trials, which can be a great way to explore their benefits without committing financially. For instance, you can try free budgeting apps before investing in premium financial tools or experiment with free fitness apps to see if they align with your goals.

Before purchasing anything, do some research. Read reviews, compare features, and think critically about how a specific tool will fit into your daily routine. Will it truly solve a problem or make your life easier? Or is it just a "nice-to-have" gadget that might end up gathering dust?

It's important that any investment you make feels intentional and aligns with your needs and lifestyle. AI tools are meant to *help*, not overwhelm. Remember, the goal isn't to accumulate more things, it's to find meaningful solutions that make your life better.

AI is our leverage for freedom

The following tables summarize the AI tools discussed in this book, organized by practical use and type. Use them as a quick reference to explore AI-driven solutions that fit your goals.

AI Tool	Practical Use	Type of Tool
Google Assistant	Scheduling and reminders	Virtual Assistant
Amazon Alexa	Organizing tasks, controlling smart devices	Virtual Assistant
Apple Siri	Voice command responses	Virtual Assistant
AnyList	Tracks items and suggests purchases	Shopping App
Out of Milk	Manages grocery lists	Shopping App
Amazon Alexa	Updates and manages shopping lists via voice commands	Virtual Assistant
Samsung Family Hub	Monitors inventory and expiration dates	Smart Refrigerator
Nest Thermostats	Automates temperature settings based on preferences	Smart Thermostat
Philips Hue Lighting	Adjusts lighting automatically to suit user routines	Smart Lighting
Ring Cameras	Enhances home security with motion detection and alerts	Smart Security Camera
Mint	Monitors spending and provides insights into expenses	Budgeting App
PocketGuard	Tracks income and spending to help users stay within budget	Financial Tracking App
YNAB (You Need a Budget)	Helps create saving plans and manage financial goals	Budgeting and Planning Tool
Betterment	Manages investments and rebalances portfolios automatically based on financial goals and market trends	Robo-Advisor
Wealthfront	Provides personalized investment strategies and automates portfolio management	Investment Management Tool
Fitbit	Tracks activity levels, sleep quality, and heart rate	Wearable Fitness Tracker
Apple Watch	Monitors health metrics, provides fitness insights, and supports wellness apps	Smartwatch with Fitness Features
WHOOP	Focuses on fitness recovery, sleep tracking, and strain monitoring	Wearable Health Tracker
Freeletics	Offers personalized workout routines based on fitness goals	Fitness App
MyFitnessPal	Tracks calorie intake, meal plans, and fitness progress	Nutrition and Fitness App
PetSafe Smart Feed	Automates pet feeding with precise portion control	Pet Feeding Device
Litter-Robot 4	Automates litter box cleaning for cats	Self-Cleaning Pet Care Device
Furbo Dog Camera	Allows remote pet monitoring with treat dispensing and bark alerts	Pet Camera and Monitor
Fi Smart Collar	Tracks pet activity, location, and health metrics	Pet Health and GPS Tracker
Whistle Health	Monitors pet health, activity levels, and behavior changes	Pet Health Monitoring

AI Tool	Practical Use	Type of Tool
Google Travel	Curates personalized itineraries and offers travel recommendations	Travel Planning Platform
Skyscanner	Finds the best flight, hotel, and car rental deals by analyzing dynamic pricing	Price Comparison and Booking Platform
Hopper	Predicts airfare and hotel price trends, sending alerts for the best booking times	Travel Savings App
Google Lens	Translates signs, menus, and text in real-time for seamless communication	Visual Translation and Recognition Tool
Google Maps	Provides real-time navigation, traffic updates, and route optimization	Navigation and Mapping Tool
LinkedIn	Personalized job recommendations and networking	Job Search and Networking
Indeed	Job postings and tailored job recommendations	Job Search Platform
Glassdoor	Job recommendations and company reviews	Job Search Platform
Interview Warmup	Simulates interview scenarios and provides feedback	AI Interview Preparation
Otter.ai	Transcribes and summarizes meetings or interviews	AI Meeting Management
AI Minutes by Avoma	Summarizes and organizes meeting content	AI Meeting Management
Fireflies.ai	Records, transcribes, and highlights key meeting points	AI Meeting Management
Zapier	Automates workflows by connecting apps	Workflow Automation Tool
Asana AI	Assigns tasks, tracks progress and suggests deadlines	Project Management and Automation Tool
Trello	Organizes projects and automates task tracking	Project Management Tool
ChatGPT	Provides conversational AI for brainstorming and writing	Generative AI for Productivity
Co-pilot	Assists in coding, writing, and task automation	AI Development and Automation Tool
Dall.e	Creates images from text descriptions	Generative AI for Design
HireVue	Analyzes and screens candidates through video interviews	AI Recruitment Tool
Greenhouse	Streamlines hiring processes with candidate evaluations	AI Recruitment Tool
LinkedIn Recruiter	Identifies and contacts potential job candidates	AI Recruitment and Networking Tool
Coursera	Offers personalized learning paths and certifications	Online Learning Platform
edX	Provides courses for upskilling and professional development	Online Learning Platform

Precautions and Limitations

AI offers remarkable benefits, transforming the way we live, work, and connect with the world. However, as with any powerful tool, it comes with challenges and risks that demand our attention and understanding. While AI has the potential to improve efficiency, enhance personalization, and simplify decision-making, it also raises questions about its limitations, responsibilities, and potential misuse.

This chapter delves into the critical aspects of using AI responsibly, focusing on areas such as data privacy, over-reliance, and ethical considerations. For instance, while AI-powered tools can streamline tasks and improve productivity, they may also lead to dependency, reducing critical thinking and problem-solving skills. Similarly, the data that fuels AI systems often raises concerns about transparency, ownership, and potential biases, which can impact fairness and inclusivity.

By exploring these limitations, this chapter aims to equip readers with the knowledge to navigate the complexities of AI adoption. It emphasizes the importance of staying informed, exercising caution, and taking proactive steps to mitigate risks. From understanding the boundaries of AI capabilities to maintaining a balanced perspective on its role in our lives, this chapter serves as a guide to integrating AI responsibly and effectively.

Data Privacy Concerns

The potential misuse of data, whether through breaches, unethical practices, or lack of transparency, highlights the importance of understanding how AI systems operate. It's no longer just about convenience; it's about control. Consumers must remain vigilant, reading privacy policies, setting data-sharing preferences, and utilizing tools to protect their digital footprint.

Data privacy isn't just a technical issue, it's a matter of trust. As AI continues to shape our daily lives, users must balance the benefits of personalization with the responsibility of protecting their information. The ability to safeguard your data empowers you to enjoy the advantages of AI without compromising your security or autonomy.

What Data Is Being Collected?
AI systems often collect a broad range of personal data, including browsing habits, location, and even sensitive health information. This data enhances AI's ability to deliver accurate recommendations and tailor user experiences but raises questions about who controls this information and how it's used.

Practical Example:
Voice-activated assistants like Google Assistant, Alexa, and Siri collect voice recordings, search history, and location data to improve

their services. However, a Statista survey reveals that 75% of users are concerned about how their data is used, often lacking clarity on protection measures.

Most AI platforms store data in centralized systems owned by companies, creating ambiguity around data ownership. Emerging solutions like personal data stores and blockchain-based decentralized storage are empowering users to take control of their information. These innovations may soon allow users to decide how their data is shared and with whom.

Steps to Protect Your Privacy
Proactive measures are essential for maintaining data privacy. Key strategies include:
o   Reviewing Privacy Settings: Regularly adjust settings on platforms like Google Assistant to limit access and delete stored voice recordings.
o   Limiting Permissions: Only grant apps the permissions they genuinely need. For example, restrict location tracking if it's not critical to app functionality.
o   Using Secure Practices: Employ strong passwords, two-factor authentication, and VPNs to secure your accounts. Encrypt cloud-stored documents for added protection.

Practical Example:

Anna, a graphic designer, uses tools like Grammarly and Google Drive. Concerned about privacy, she reviews permissions frequently, encrypts her files, and uses a password manager. Research from the Identity Theft Resource Center shows these habits significantly reduce the risk of unauthorized data access.

Emerging Privacy Regulations

Global frameworks like the GDPR in Europe and the CCPA in California are empowering users with greater control over their data. For instance, GDPR provides the "right to be forgotten" and requires explicit consent for data collection. Understanding these regulations helps users exercise their rights and navigate AI tools responsibly.

The Risks of Over-Reliance on AI

Over-reliance on AI carries a range of risks that, if unchecked, can impact individuals, organizations, and even society at large. While AI brings incredible convenience and efficiency, it's important to recognize its limitations and avoid placing blind faith in its capabilities.

One major risk is the erosion of critical human skills. When AI takes over tasks like decision-making, problem-solving, and even communication, we risk losing essential abilities like creativity, critical thinking, and emotional intelligence. These skills are foundational to human adaptability and innovation, and neglecting them could hinder personal and societal growth over time.

Another concern is reduced accountability. Over-reliance on AI can lead to a mindset where users trust the technology to the extent that they no longer feel responsible for the outcomes. When something goes wrong, it becomes easy to point fingers at the AI system rather than reflecting on human oversight or decision-making failures. This issue becomes particularly troubling in areas where ethical judgment is crucial, such as hiring, law enforcement, or healthcare. AI systems, though powerful, lack the nuanced understanding of human values and context, which can result in decisions that inadvertently perpetuate biases or unfair outcomes.

Additionally, overconfidence in AI's capabilities can be risky. Many people assume that AI systems are infallible, but in reality, they are only as good as the data they are trained on. AI can misinterpret or fail to handle rare or complex scenarios, leading to errors with significant consequences. This overconfidence can lead to a "hands-off" approach, where human oversight is reduced, particularly in critical sectors like aviation or healthcare. Such over-automation can be catastrophic if the AI system fails or encounters a situation it wasn't designed to handle.

Dependence on AI also creates vulnerabilities to manipulation. As we integrate AI more deeply into our lives, malicious actors have greater opportunities to exploit this reliance. From hacking AI systems to spreading misinformation or biasing algorithms, the potential for harm grows with our increasing dependence on these tools. Blind trust in AI can make individuals and organizations easy targets for cyberattacks or scams.

Another long-term risk is stagnation in human innovation. AI is a tool that thrives on existing data, but its ability to think creatively or outside the box is limited. If we rely entirely on AI for innovation, we risk losing the imaginative and unconventional problem-solving that drives breakthroughs. Human ingenuity remains essential for advancing knowledge and pushing boundaries in ways that AI cannot replicate.

By understanding these risks, we can use AI wisely, ensuring it complements rather than replaces human capabilities. The goal should be to strike a balance: leveraging AI to improve efficiency and productivity while maintaining human oversight, accountability, and the essential skills that make us unique. When approached thoughtfully, AI can serve as a powerful ally, but only if we remain conscious of its limitations and our role in guiding its use responsibly.

The Balance Between Automation and Human Skills

AI excels at automating repetitive tasks, but critical decisions require human judgment, ethics, and intuition, qualities that AI cannot replicate. For example, while an AI might optimize a business decision for cost, it might not fully consider its ethical implications.

Practical Example:
Tom, a financial advisor, uses robo-advisors to manage client portfolios. During market turbulence, he advises clients against rash decisions, complementing AI's short-term focus with his expertise. Studies show that blending human judgment with AI tools enhances decision quality and client satisfaction.

Addressing AI Dependency

Over-reliance on AI can weaken problem-solving and interpersonal skills. Practicing "digital mindfulness", deciding when to rely on AI and when to engage independently, helps maintain a healthy balance.

Cross-Checking AI Information

AI systems, though efficient, can make errors or exhibit biases. Cross-checking AI-generated information is essential, especially in fields like healthcare and finance where errors can have significant consequences.

Practical Example:

Sophie uses an AI-powered health app for symptom analysis. While she trusts the app for minor issues, she consults her doctor for more serious concerns. The WHO recommends treating AI healthcare tools as aids, not replacements for professional advice.

> **AI "Black Box" Issues**
>
> Many AI systems operate as "black boxes," where decision-making processes are opaque. This is particularly problematic in fields like criminal justice and healthcare. Transparency and human oversight are critical to addressing these limitations.

Ethical Considerations

As AI advances introduces ethical dilemmas that challenge our societal norms. From algorithmic bias and job displacement to questions surrounding privacy, accountability, and even autonomy, these issues demand careful scrutiny to ensure that AI benefits humanity as a whole. To provide deeper insight and foster a balanced perspective, this sub-chapter incorporates quotes and opinions from specialists who are at the forefront of AI ethics and innovation.

Algorithmic Bias

At its core, AI relies on data. However, this dependence can also be its greatest weakness. As noted by computer scientist **Joy Buolamwini**, founder of the Algorithmic Justice League,

> "Bias in AI systems is not a technical issue, it's a societal one. If the data reflects inequalities, so will the algorithms."

Algorithmic bias has manifested in various forms, from hiring tools that favor certain demographics to facial recognition systems with higher error rates for minorities. The infamous case of an AI hiring system penalizing female applicants due to historical male-dominated hiring practices serves as a stark reminder that AI can perpetuate, and even amplify, societal prejudices.

Addressing this challenge requires both transparency and accountability. AI developers must implement continuous audits and emphasize ethical design practices to reduce biases. Philosopher **Nick Bostrom**, a leading voice in AI ethics, speculates that

> "unchecked AI could encode values that conflict with humanity's well-being."

The key, as he posits, is aligning AI's goals with human ethics to avoid unintended consequences.

Job Displacement

The debate surrounding AI's impact on employment is as old as technological disruption itself. Historically, automation has eliminated certain jobs while creating entirely new ones. For instance, factory automation replaced manual labor, but it gave rise to roles in engineering and maintenance. However, AI's rapid development now challenges white-collar jobs once considered untouchable. **Kai-Fu Lee**, renowned AI expert and author of *AI Superpowers*, predicts that

> "AI will automate 40% of jobs within 15 years."

From legal document reviews to medical diagnostics, AI's efficiency is unmatched.

While this shift promises increased productivity, it also raises questions about economic disparity and reskilling. Will AI leave entire populations behind, or will it enable society to explore new opportunities? Futurists argue that governments and corporations must collaborate on reskilling initiatives to prepare workers for a new AI-driven economy. **Yuval Noah Harari**, who envisions AI as a tool to reduce work hours and enhance human creativity, if used responsibly.

Privacy and Data Security: Who Owns Your Information?

The rise of AI is synonymous with the rise of big data. From health records to social media behavior, AI systems require enormous amounts of personal information to operate effectively. However, this dependency raises concerns about privacy breaches and data ownership. Edward Snowden, known for his advocacy of privacy rights, has warned, "AI magnifies the ability to surveil individuals on an unprecedented scale. The question is: Who's watching the watchers?"

As companies and governments collect and monetize user data, individuals risk losing control over their digital footprints. **Elon Musk**, CEO of Tesla and OpenAI co-founder, underscores the need for regulations, suggesting that

> "AI is more dangerous than nuclear weapons if left unchecked."

Musk advocates for ethical frameworks and transparency to ensure AI respects individual privacy while delivering societal benefits.

Autonomy and Accountability: Who's Responsible?

As AI becomes more sophisticated, questions surrounding autonomy and accountability grow louder. When an autonomous vehicle causes an accident or an AI healthcare system provides flawed diagnoses, who is to blame? These ethical dilemmas force us to rethink legal and moral frameworks. Legal scholar **Ryan Calo** suggests that current systems lack the flexibility to assign responsibility when decisions are made by algorithms rather than humans.

Moreover, AI's potential to achieve "superintelligence", a concept explored by Nick Bostrom, raises fears of losing control over machines. While this remains speculative, Bostrom warns, "The first superintelligent AI could also be the last invention we make, if we fail to instill safeguards and values aligned with human welfare."

The Path Forward: Ethical AI for the Future
The ethical concerns surrounding AI are complex and multi-faceted. However, ignoring these challenges risks undermining the benefits AI can provide. Solutions lie in:

- **Ethical Governance:** Policymakers must create global frameworks to regulate AI development, ensuring fairness, transparency, and accountability.
- **Inclusive AI Development:** Diverse teams and ethical audits can minimize algorithmic biases and promote equitable outcomes.
- **Human-Centric AI:** As Harari suggests, "The ultimate goal of AI should be to enhance human capabilities, not replace them."

Ultimately, ethical AI is not just a technical challenge, it is a societal one. As we stand at the threshold of an AI-driven future, our ability to navigate these moral questions will determine whether AI becomes humanity's greatest ally or its most dangerous adversary.

> Ethics in AI is not about halting progress, it's about ensuring progress serves everyone. "The coded gaze can be inclusive, but only if we make it so."
>
> By Joy Buolamwini

Algorithmic Bias and Fairness

AI is only as impartial as the data it's trained on. Biased datasets can reinforce inequalities, particularly in hiring, finance, and law enforcement.

Practical Example:

Some companies use AI for resume screening, but biased training data has led to favoritism, such as preferring male candidates. Incorporating human oversight helps mitigate these biases, as highlighted by MIT Technology Review.

Job Automation and Displacement

While AI creates efficiencies, it also raises concerns about job displacement. Reskilling and upskilling are critical to preparing the workforce for AI-driven transformations.

Practical Example:
Jack, a factory worker, faced automation in his role but adapted by training to operate and maintain AI systems. A PwC report emphasizes that companies must prioritize workforce reskilling to complement AI adoption.

Technology should liberate us, not replace us

Yuval Noah Harari

Ethical Dilemma	Description	Example	Why It Matters
Algorithmic Bias	AI systems inherit biases from training data, leading to unfair or discriminatory outcomes.	A hiring tool may favor men over women due to biased historical employment data.	Bias can perpetuate societal inequities, particularly in hiring, law enforcement, and lending.
Job Displacement	AI automation replaces human workers, especially in repetitive or manual roles.	Self-checkout systems and autonomous trucks reduce the need for cashiers and drivers.	Widespread job loss can increase economic inequality and leave low-skilled workers behind.
Privacy and Surveillance	AI relies on personal data, raising concerns about privacy and intrusive surveillance.	Social media platforms use AI to analyze user behavior, leading to misuse (e.g., Cambridge Analytica).	Loss of personal privacy and misuse of data can undermine freedom and trust.
Accountability	AI errors or failures make it unclear who is responsible, developers, users, or the AI.	If an autonomous car causes an accident, it's unclear whether the fault lies with the AI or manufacturer.	Ambiguity in accountability can delay justice and reduce trust in AI systems.
Misinformation & Deepfakes	AI generates false content like deepfakes or propaganda that manipulates public opinion.	Deepfake videos of public figures spread misinformation and deceive viewers.	False content undermines trust in media, democracy, and public discourse.
AI in Warfare	Autonomous weapons make life-or-death decisions without human intervention.	AI-powered drones autonomously identify and strike targets.	Reduces human accountability in warfare and risks civilian harm.
Human Dependence	Over-reliance on AI erodes human skills like creativity, problem-solving, and critical thinking.	Automated tools for communication or navigation reduce independent human engagement.	Excessive reliance on AI risks reducing innovation, autonomy, and resilience.
Data Ownership	Ambiguity over who owns the data used by AI systems, particularly user-generated data.	Generative AI tools train on publicly available content, infringing on creators' intellectual property.	Raises ethical questions about consent, ownership, and compensation.
Lack of Transparency	AI decision-making can be a "black box," making it difficult to understand or challenge results.	Credit scoring AI may deny loans without explaining the reasoning behind its decisions.	Transparency is critical for fairness, trust, and accountability in AI-driven systems.
Ethical Decision-Making	AI making moral decisions raises questions about whose values are encoded into systems.	Autonomous vehicles face moral dilemmas like the "trolley problem"—choosing between passengers and pedestrians.	Moral frameworks vary globally, complicating AI design and ethical alignment.

Future

As we look toward the years 2030 to 2035, the role of artificial intelligence will become even more intertwined with our lives. AI is no longer just a helpful tool, it's set to become a seamless partner in how we manage health, work, homes, finances, and even how we care for our pets. Experts and futurists predict technologies that sound like science fiction today will be commonplace tomorrow, pushing boundaries and redefining how we live.

While some of these ideas remain speculative, they reflect trends already emerging in labs, tech companies, and design studios around the globe. Let's explore what the coming years could bring and how AI will transform our everyday lives.

Health and Fitness: AI as Your Personal Doctor and Coach

By 2035, healthcare will see AI-powered tools that make personal health monitoring feel like second nature. Imagine wearing a "Smart Health Patch 2.0", an invisible skin sensor that monitors your blood pressure, hydration, and organ health 24/7. It could detect illnesses weeks before symptoms show up, giving you preventive treatment options well in advance. Companies like Apple, Google, and Fitbit are already heading in this direction, but in the next decade, we'll see far more advanced iterations.

For fitness enthusiasts, the rise of Virtual AI Trainers like *FitAura* will completely transform home workouts. Instead of generic videos or static apps, *FitAura* will use holographic technology to create a lifelike trainer that monitors your form, corrects posture, and adapts workouts based on real-time data like heart rate or fatigue levels. Whether you're a beginner or elite athlete, your AI coach will ensure maximum results while reducing injuries.

Home Chores: Meet the Next Generation of House Robots

The future of home management lies in the rise of multifunctional household robots. Today, we have robotic vacuums like Roombas, but by 2035, these devices will be fully autonomous helpers capable of performing complex tasks. Meet *Rosie 3.0*, a smart home robot that folds your laundry, washes dishes, and even restocks your pantry by connecting to AI-powered grocery services. Companies like Samsung and Amazon are already experimenting with early versions, such as Ballie and Astro, hinting at what's to come.

What makes *Rosie 3.0* even smarter is her ability to learn your preferences. She'll organize your home in ways that match your routine, like sorting shoes at the front door or making sure your coffee is ready before you even wake up. However, experts warn that such powerful robots raise new safety and privacy risks, especially if they malfunction or collect sensitive data.

Jobs and Work-Life Balance: AI Co-Workers and 4-Day Workweek
The workplace of 2030-2035 will see AI taking on far more responsibilities, allowing us to reclaim time for ourselves. Tools like *WorkMate AI*, an upgraded version of today's Microsoft Co-pilot or ChatGPT, will autonomously handle entire projects, from researching reports to creating presentations and summarizing team meetings.

This shift could pave the way for shorter workweeks, a concept long discussed by futurists and tech leaders. With AI-driven automation increasing productivity, many believe the 4-day workweek could become standard. Imagine having Fridays free to pursue hobbies, spend time with loved ones, or simply recharge.

Finance: AI That Grows Your Wealth Automatically
By 2035, managing your finances will feel almost effortless. AI-powered tools like WealthBots will handle savings, investments, and debt reduction entirely on autopilot. These tools will analyze global economic trends in real-time, helping you grow your money faster and with fewer risks.

Budgeting will evolve, too. Tools like AI Wallets will anticipate your financial behavior and send alerts, like, "If you skip that extra coffee today, you'll hit your savings goal for your dream trip next month." This level of financial foresight will empower users to make smarter decisions without constant effort.

Pet Care: AI Companions Keeping Furry Friends Happy

Caring for pets will also benefit from AI-driven advancements. By 2035, robotic companions like *PawPal* will play with your pets, keep them active, and monitor their health. *PawPal* will use built-in cameras, toys, and smart sensors to create tailored play sessions, ensuring your pet stays engaged while you're at work or away.

On the health front, AI Vet Monitors will analyze your pet's behavior and vital signs with astonishing precision. If your dog's activity drops suddenly or if their eating habits change, these tools will send alerts, helping you catch health issues before they escalate.

Travel and Holidays: Seamless and Stress-Free Adventures

The way we plan and experience holidays will be revolutionized too. Tools like AI Travel Planners will create hyper-personalized itineraries tailored to your preferences, budget, and travel history. Instead of spending hours browsing flights, accommodations, and attractions, AI platforms will design the perfect trip in seconds, booking everything for you.

Imagine stepping into an airport where facial recognition systems replace tickets and passports, making check-ins and security lines virtually seamless. Smart airports, powered by AI, will predict passenger flows, reducing wait times by up to 50%. Once at your destination, real-time translation apps will allow you to converse in any language naturally, breaking down barriers and making travel more immersive.

Virtual reality (VR) powered by AI will even enable travelers to preview destinations before booking. For instance, you could take a virtual stroll through Tokyo's Shibuya Crossing or gaze at Santorini's sunsets from your living room.

However, some futurists predict that fully autonomous travel robots, like TravelBot 3000, will serve as your *personal tour guide*. These devices could carry your bags, capture photos, and even help you navigate crowded streets, ensuring stress-free holidays. Yet, as with other AI tools, privacy concerns arise, how much personal data will these bots collect?

The years to come promise to be an era of unprecedented advancements. From smart health patches that predict illnesses to house robots managing every chore, AI will free us from repetitive tasks and empower us to focus on what truly matters.
Travel will become more seamless, holidays more immersive, and our lives more balanced. The vision is clear: AI will help us live smarter, healthier, and more fulfilling lives. But as we stand at the edge of this exciting future, we must remain mindful, balancing the convenience of AI with the responsibility to use it ethically and wisely.

Conclusion

Artificial Intelligence is no longer a thing of the future or just a passing trend, it's already part of our everyday lives. Whether it's helping you stay organized, improving healthcare, managing your money, or planning a vacation, AI is here to make life easier and more efficient.

The beauty of AI lies in its potential to give us back our most precious resource: time. Time to focus on family, creativity, personal growth, or simply enjoying the little moments we so often overlook. While AI tools can seem overwhelming at first, the truth is, you don't need to be a tech wizard or adopt every innovation out there. Start small. Find the areas where AI can truly make a difference for *you*, and let it amplify what matters most in your life.

That's what this book has been about, to show you the possibilities AI brings while encouraging you to stay intentional, curious, and informed. As with any tool, the real magic happens when we use it with purpose. AI isn't here to replace us. Instead, it's a way to empower us, helping us make smarter decisions, live more efficiently, and unlock opportunities we never imagined.

So whether you're looking for ways to save time, improve your health, or enhance your career, know this: AI is not just for scientists or big corporations. It's for all of us, everyday people, with busy lives, big dreams, and a desire for a little more balance.

As we close this book, we hope you feel inspired to embrace AI in your own way. Remember, the future isn't something that happens to us. It's something we shape, step by step, choice by choice. Let AI be your leverage for freedom, creativity, and a life filled with more of what you love.

Final toughts

It's both fascinating and unsettling how much robots, AI, and the internet already know about us. Picture this: you're sitting in your favorite café, ready to indulge in a chocolate croissant or that tempting extra latte, and suddenly, your smartwatch nudges you with a warning, "Maybe skip the chocolate today; your calorie count is already high." Or perhaps your finance app sends a gentle reminder, "Remember your budget - do you really need that second coffee?" These are small nudges, seemingly harmless, but they highlight just how much these systems know about our habits, our preferences, and even our weaknesses.

The eerie part? They don't stop there. AI can predict where you'll go next, not because you told it, but because it's been quietly piecing together your routines. Maybe it listened to your conversations (was that ad for a new gym membership really just a coincidence?) or noticed you searched for running shoes yesterday and assumed a fitness phase is on the horizon. These systems learn from the smallest breadcrumbs of your behavior, whether it's tracking your location, listening to keywords, or analyzing how long you pause on a social media post. It's like having an invisible assistant that knows you, sometimes better than you know yourself.

On one hand, we appreciate this level of personalization. It simplifies life, saves us time, and makes our choices easier. AI knows our favorite routes, suggests movies we'll love, and even reminds us when to drink water or stand up. It's convenient, and let's be honest, many of us love the efficiency it brings. Who wouldn't want their life fine-tuned to perfection with minimal effort?

But here's the other side of the coin, the side that feels a little too close for comfort. Are we giving up too much of ourselves for this convenience? With every click, swipe, and voice command, we're feeding a system that builds an increasingly accurate picture of our lives. It knows where we've been, what we buy, who we talk to, what we like, and even what we might want next. How much of our personal freedom and identity are we sacrificing when we willingly allow machines to anticipate our needs and desires?

It's worth asking: if AI does so much of the thinking for us, what happens to who we are? When we no longer decide for ourselves, whether it's what to eat, where to go, or how to spend our money, do we risk losing touch with our instincts, our individuality, and even our sense of self? This trade-off isn't just about privacy; it's about autonomy and identity.

In a world where AI seems to know our every move before we make it, we have to pause and ask: how much control are we comfortable giving up? And more importantly, who is really in control, us or the machines we've invited into our lives? It's a balancing act, one that forces us to reflect on the boundaries we're willing to set in exchange for the ease and precision AI offers. Because while it's comforting to have machines understand us so well, it's equally critical to ensure we don't lose ourselves in the process.

References

General AI Concepts and History
1. Russell, S., & Norvig, P. (2020). *Artificial Intelligence: A Modern Approach* (4th ed.). Pearson.
2. IBM Research Blog. (Various). *Deep Blue and Watson Case Studies*. IBM.
3. Silver, D., et al. (2016). *Mastering the Game of Go with Deep Neural Networks and Tree Search*. Nature, 529(7587), 484-489.

Statistics on AI Adoption and Growth
1. McKinsey Global Institute. (2017). *Artificial Intelligence: The Next Digital Frontier?*
2. Statista. (2021). *Global AI Market Size & Revenue Forecast*. Retrieved from https://www.statista.com
3. Salesforce. (2020). *State of the Connected Customer*.

AI in Daily Life
1. Netflix Technology Blog. (2017). *The Netflix Recommender System: Algorithms, Business Value, and Innovation*. Retrieved from https://about.netflix.com
2. Spotify Engineering Blog. (2015). *How Spotify Curates Your Discover Weekly Playlist*, by Edward Newett and Trevor Lamkin. Retrieved from https://engineering.atspotify.com
3. Betterment. (2022). *Automated Investing with Betterment*. Retrieved from https://www.betterment.com

4. Fitbit. (2022). *The Science Behind Fitbit Sleep Tracking*. Fitbit, Inc. Retrieved from https://www.fitbit.com

5. Harvard Health Publishing. (2020). *Do Fitness Trackers Really Improve Your Health?* Harvard Medical School.

6. BMJ (British Medical Journal). (2020). *The Potential of AI-Assisted Healthcare for Symptom Assessment.*

7. Todoist Blog. (Various). *Productivity Tool Insights*. Retrieved from https://todoist.com/blog

8. RescueTime Blog. (2022). *The Impact of Time Tracking on Productivity*. Retrieved from https://www.rescuetime.com

9. Otter.ai. (2021). *AI-Powered Transcription for Enhanced Productivity*. Retrieved from https://otter.ai

10. American Council for an Energy-Efficient Economy (ACEEE). (2020). *Smart Home Technologies and Energy Efficiency.*

Precautions and Limitations of AI

1. Electronic Frontier Foundation (EFF). (2021). *Privacy and Data Security Concerns in AI*. Retrieved from https://www.eff.org

2. European Commission. (2018). *General Data Protection Regulation (GDPR)*. Retrieved from https://eur-lex.europa.eu

3. O'Neil, C. (2016). *Weapons of Math Destruction: How Big Data Increases Inequality and Threatens Democracy*. Crown Publishing.

Ethical Considerations

1. PwC. (2018). *Will Robots Really Steal Our Jobs?* Retrieved from https://www.pwc.com

2. OECD. (2019). *The Future of Work and AI*. OECD Publishing.

3. European Union. (2021). *The EU AI Act: A Legal Framework for Artificial Intelligence*. European Commission. Retrieved from https://digital-strategy.ec.europa.eu

Legal Disclaimer

This book was developed with the assistance of artificial intelligence (AI) tools for research, drafting, and organizational support. While the content represents a synthesis of publicly available information, industry knowledge, and established concepts in the field of Artificial Intelligence, AI tools were used to streamline the drafting process, organize references, and enhance readability. All interpretations, opinions, and conclusions presented herein are those of the author and do not necessarily reflect the views of any AI technology provider.

The authors made every effort to ensure accuracy and reliability, relying on a combination of trusted sources, industry standards, and personal expertise. However, AI tools have inherent limitations and should not be viewed as a substitute for professional advice or independent research. The authors encourage readers to consult primary sources and use discretion when applying any information from this book in personal or professional contexts.

www.ingramcontent.com/pod-product-compliance
Lightning Source LLC
Chambersburg PA
CBHW070202230526
45471CB00002B/790